It's a Family Thanksgiving!

*A Celebration of an American Tradition
for Children and Their Families*

Deborah F. Fink, M.A.
Illustrated by Kinny Kreiswirth

Harmony Hearth, LLC

This book is dedicated to my family tree: To my children, my husband, my mother, my grandparents, and my immigrant great-grandparents, who worked hard to achieve the American dream for their children, their children's children, and their grandchildren's children.

All my endeavors are in honor of my beloved sister, whose memory carries me to unknown territories and whose loving touch moves through me forever.
– DFF

Text © 2000, 1996 by
Deborah F. Fink
Illustrations © 2000 by
Kinny Kreiswirth

Published by
HARMONY HEARTH, LLC,
Bethesda, Md.
www.harmonyhearth.com
Printed in Canada

ISBN 0-9678871-0-0

I would like to dedicate this book to my family, both immediate and extended, who have roots in England, Scotland, France, Holland, Poland, and Russia, from as early as the 1600s to as recently as the 1900s. They have all given us every reason to be thankful.
– KK

A percentage of the proceeds from the sale of this book will be donated to not-for-profit organizations that work to improve the quality of life for less-privileged children and youth.

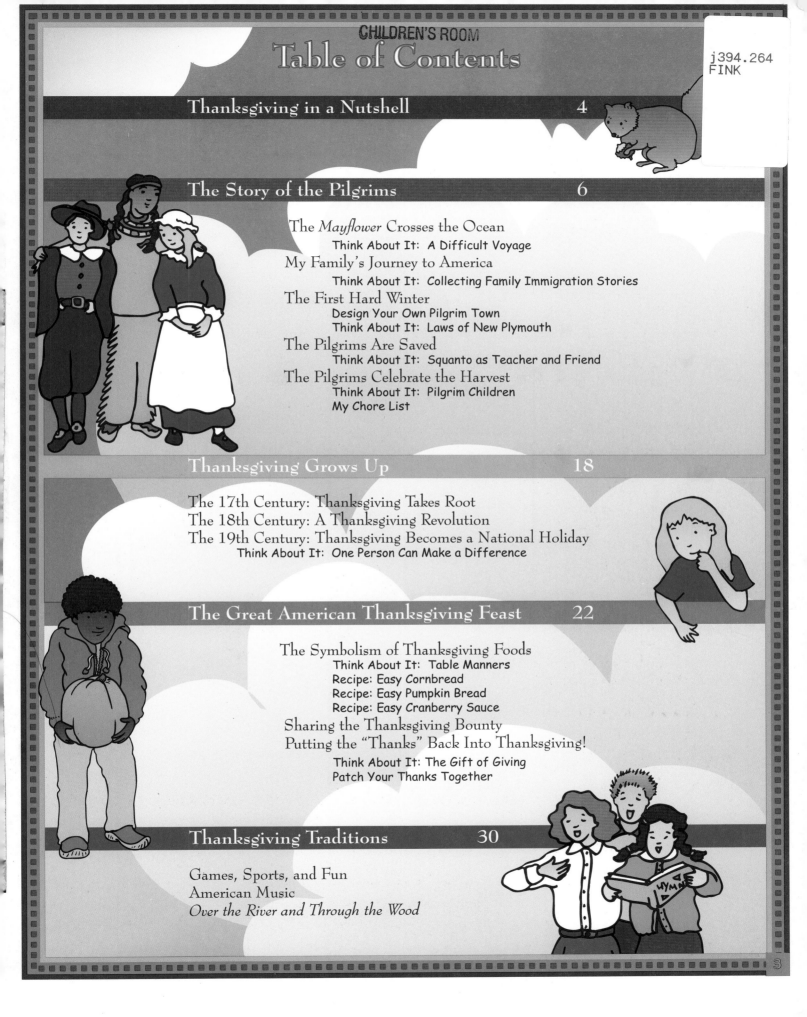

Table of Contents

Thanksgiving in a Nutshell

Every year, on the fourth Thursday in November, Americans come together to celebrate Thanksgiving. Families gather from far and wide. Turkeys are cooked and pumpkin pies are baked. Games and sports are played. Songs are sung. Prayers of thanks are offered. It's a tradition that goes back nearly 400 years. And you're a part of it, just like all of the American boys and girls who have come before you.

The cornucopia has become a symbol of Thanksgiving. It is shaped like a curved goat's horn that is overflowing with fruit, flowers, and corn. It symbolizes abundance, prosperity, and the bounty of the earth. Also called a horn of plenty, a cornucopia represents plenty of food and drink. (Cornucopia is also a great word for a spelling bee!)

But where did this great tradition come from?

Legend has it that the first Thanksgiving took place in the fall of 1621. It happened at a tiny settlement called Plymouth on the coast of what is now Massachusetts. English settlers who called themselves Pilgrims invited their Native American neighbors to a great feast to celebrate the first harvest in their new home in America.

Place your Thanksgiving family photo here.

My Thanksgiving
2_____

Age: _____

Grade: _____

I'm celebrating Thanksgiving at:

_____

I'm celebrating Thanksgiving with:

_____

_____

_____

The spirit of the Pilgrims has survived for close to four centuries. Although hundreds of years have passed, we still remember that first harvest celebration every time we sit down with friends and family for our own Thanksgiving dinner.

And so our story begins. . .

The Story

NOVA BRITANNIA
OFFERING
most excellent
FRUITES
by planting in
VIRGINIA
Exciting all Such as be well
affected to further the Same.

LONDON
Printed for
SAMVEL MACHEM,
and are to be Sold at his Shop
in Pauls Church-yard,
at the Signe of the Bul-head,
1 6 0 9.

Long ago, in the early 1600s, a strict king named James I ruled England. He commanded his subjects to join the Church of England and follow its religious rules. But not everyone was happy with the way the Church of England worshiped God, including a group of religious people called Puritans. Some of the Puritans wanted to completely separate from the king's church to worship God in their own way. They were called Separatists.

King James made it clear that there wasn't room in his country for other religions. He decided to make life very hard for the Separatists, in the hope that they would eventually leave England.

In 1608, some of the Separatists decided to escape to Holland, where all kinds of beliefs were welcome. At first, they liked Holland and the Dutch people. But some Separatist parents started to worry that if they stayed in Holland their children would stop being real Englishmen. So a group of them decided to look for a place that would let them practice their religion but would still be English. There was only one place they could go: The brand-new colonies in North America.

of the Pilgrims

The leader of the group that decided to leave Holland was William Bradford. He gave his small group of Separatists a special name before they left. He called them Pilgrims, a word that means people on a religious journey.

The Pilgrims were poor and couldn't afford to cross the ocean on their own. Luckily, they soon found some businessmen who would help pay for the trip. The Pilgrims agreed to a business deal and got permission to settle in the English colony known as Virginia.

There was one more problem: Only about 40 Pilgrims wanted to go. That wasn't enough to fill up the ship or to make the voyage worthwhile. So other people who wanted to start new lives in the mysterious world across the ocean came, too. The Pilgrims called these people "strangers." The Pilgrims were happy to have the strangers join them, as long as the Pilgrims stayed in charge.

Finally, in mid-September of 1620, a collection of 102 passengers crowded onto one little ship. The passengers included the 40 Pilgrims, over 40 officers and crew, many strangers, two dogs, and other animals. The name of the ship was the *Mayflower*—and it would soon change the world.

Draw symbolic decorations for the sails of the Mayflower. For example, the Pilgrims may have depicted a flower, a cross, a bird, or a fish.

The *Mayflower* Crosses the Ocean

The long voyage was very difficult. The ship was very crowded, cold, and smelly. There was little food, and icy winter storms tossed the little boat around. It must have been a very tough voyage for the boys and girls on board.

At last, about two months later, the crew sighted land. The trip had taken 65 cold and painful days. Everyone was glad to finally see the coast of America. They quickly discovered, though, that they weren't in the right place. Instead of Virginia, they found themselves at Cape Cod, in what is now Massachusetts. They were hundreds of miles too far north!

It was too late to do anything about it. They were tired and worried about running out of food. Almost everyone agreed that even though they didn't have permission, they would land on Cape Cod anyway. They decided to make the best of a bad situation.

For a month they sailed around Cape Cod looking for a good place to build a village. Finally, in mid-December, they discovered a site that looked promising. They sent a few explorers ashore to take a look. It was a spot that already had some cleared land where a Native American village had once stood. They called the place Plymouth, after the English port they had left over three months earlier. The women and children stayed on board the *Mayflower* with their belongings. The men left the ship to begin building their new life in an unfamiliar, dangerous, and harsh land.

THINK ABOUT IT: A Difficult Voyage

The Pilgrims' voyage on the **Mayflower** was cold, dangerous, and crowded. All the space on the ship was filled with supplies for the long journey. There wasn't much room for personal items, especially for the children. They knew they would have to start their lives over once they got to America.

Pretend you're a child on a ship like the **Mayflower**. If you could only bring what you could carry in a small bag, what would you take?

_____

_____

_____

_____

_____

What would be the most difficult things for you to leave behind?

_____

_____

_____

_____

_____

THINK ABOUT IT: Collecting Family Immigration Stories

This Thanksgiving you can be the family historian. You will probably be celebrating Thanksgiving with people who know many stories about your family's immigration. Collect these stories. You just need to ask the right questions to find out important information: Where did they emigrate (leave) from? Why did they leave? When did they arrive in America? Where did they settle? How did they travel (by foot, horse, ship, car, train or plane)? If your heritage is Native American, where did your ancestors live when the Europeans arrived? To which people did they belong?

Why did your family members decide to come to America?

Check their different reasons:

- [ ] to escape persecution (like the Pilgrims)
- [ ] to seek adventure or their fortunes (like the "strangers")
- [ ] to join a loved one
- [ ] to work as a slave or servant
- [ ] to escape famine or poverty
- [ ] to earn a living
- [ ] to study at a university
- [ ] to receive medical assistance
- [ ] to make a better life
- [ ] other: _____
  _____
  _____

Draw a face or paste a photo of a family member who first came to America in the four frames, and write the name below.

Europe

Asia

Indian
Ocean

Africa

Pacific
Ocean

Australia

Atlantic
Ocean

My Family's Journey to America

Help celebrate the spirit of Thanksgiving
by remembering your family's journey!

Trace your family's journey to America on this map. Draw a
line from where your mom's and/or dad's family came from
to the place in the United States where they first arrived.
Choose one color for each side of your family.

PLYMOUTH

🐋 Design Your Own Pilgrim Town

Imagine that you have just landed at Plymouth. It is the middle of winter. You are hungry and tired. You know you have to start building a place to live. What would you do?

Pretend you are the town planner. Design your plan for the first Pilgrim town below. Think about what your town will need. What would you build first? How would you arrange the town? What would you need besides buildings in order to survive? Don't forget to leave a place for your first Thanksgiving feast!

The First Hard Winter

The Pilgrims had managed to survive the difficult ocean voyage, but now found themselves in the middle of a frigid New England winter. The weather was much colder than anything they were used to back home. They were running out of food on the ship and they didn't have any boats or nets to fish. They also didn't know how to gather food in this strange new place.

Right away, they built a few simple buildings to shelter them from the bitter weather. It was hard work and took a long time. Even with the shelter of the *Mayflower*, the first winter was a nightmare. By its end only 55 of the original 102 passengers were still alive. The rest had died, mainly from pneumonia or scurvy. Scurvy is a disease caused by not eating enough fruits and vegetables. (They had none to eat.) The Pilgrims needed to figure out how to get food soon, or they would all die. It turned out that the answer to their prayers had been there all along.

THINK ABOUT IT: Laws of New Plymouth

While still on board ship, the male Pilgrims and strangers wrote and signed a document called the **Mayflower** Compact. This document said that the people would make their own government and create fair and equal laws. At this time, although they did not all agree, the men elected John Carver as their first governor.

Pretend you are Governor Carver. What "fair and equal" laws would you insist on having in your new town?

_____

_____

_____

_____

_____

_____

_____

What do you think about the fact that Pilgrim women were not allowed to sign the **Mayflower** Compact—or vote for their governor?

Squanto was both teacher and friend to the Pilgrim children, too. He showed them how to help with the farming, fishing, hunting, and gathering. Squanto the farmer taught children to protect the cornfields from hungry animals by throwing stones to scare them away. Squanto the fisherman helped children learn to use large seashells as scoops to move sand and soil. Squanto the hunter showed them where raccoons and skunks liked to hide. The older boys were responsible for hunting these smaller animals, which could be carried home without help. Squanto the gatherer taught children how and where to find cranberries, strawberries, blueberries, and other fruits and nuts. Children enjoyed gathering and eating the berries and nuts. Learning from Squanto must have been one adventurous game of hide-and-go-seek!

Do you think the Pilgrim children were thankful that they had found such a helpful teacher and friend?
Yes / No
Has anyone ever helped you the way Squanto helped the Pilgrims?
Yes / No
Have you ever helped someone or taught them something?
Yes / No
There are small and big ways of being helpful. List a few helpful things you have done recently, or a few helpful things you will do very soon.

_____

_____

_____

_____

_____

The Pilgrims Are Saved

In the spring, the ship and its crew went back to England. The survivors were left behind. But they weren't alone. Native Americans (once called Indians) lived all around them, watching and waiting to see what the Pilgrims would do. Once in a while the settlers would see or hear Native Americans in the woods. They didn't know what to expect.

It must have been quite a shock one March day when all of a sudden a Native American walked right into the Pilgrims' little village. The Pilgrims must have been even more amazed when he started speaking English!

His name was Samoset and he was a member of the Wampanoag tribe. The land where the settlers had built Plymouth had once been a village belonging to the Pawtuxet band of the Wampanoag tribe. The Pilgrims learned from Samoset that the village had been wiped out by a European disease four years earlier.

Samoset knew of a Pawtuxet who spoke English well, and introduced him to the settlers. His name was Tisquantum, but the Pilgrims called him Squanto. Squanto was the only member of the Pawtuxet band that was still alive. He understood English because he had been taken to England by a British sea captain and had lived there for many years. At another time in his life, Squanto was captured and taken to Spain as a slave, but he eventually escaped.

Because Squanto spoke English so well, he was able to serve as a translator between the Pilgrims and the local Native Americans. Squanto helped the Pilgrims communicate with the great Wampanoag chief, Massasoit. The Pilgrims eventually signed a peace treaty with Massasoit. Sadly, peace between the neighbors lasted for only one generation.

Since Squanto was all alone, he decided to live with the Pilgrims and to show them how to survive in this new land. Squanto saved the Pilgrims' lives by teaching them how to farm, fish, hunt, and gather. *Squanto the farmer* introduced the Pilgrims to Indian corn (called maize), pumpkins, and beans. They had never seen these foods in England. In fact, the Pilgrims came to call corn, pumpkins, and beans the

"Indian Three Sisters" because they were the Native Americans' three main crops. Squanto taught them how to plant the corn and fertilize the ground with dead fish. He showed them how to plant pumpkins between the cornstalks because pumpkin vines kept away weeds. He also explained how to grow beans next to the corn so their vines would climb right up the cornstalks. He was a very

clever farmer.

Squanto the fisherman taught the Pilgrims how to dig up clams along the shore, and new ways to catch lobster, cod, and other fish from the ocean. *Squanto the hunter* showed the Pilgrims how, where, and when to hunt for animals, including bears, wild turkeys, and deer. The Pilgrims learned that deer lived in valleys and roamed at sunrise and sundown, so that was when to hunt for them. *Squanto the gatherer* led the Pilgrims to edible berries, nutritious nuts, and medicinal plants.

Squanto was the Pilgrims' teacher and friend. He helped save their lives and made sure their little settlement survived in the rocky New England soil. By saving the Pilgrims, Squanto became one of our first American heroes.

The Pilgrims Celebrate the Harvest . . . .

The men, women, and children who had lived through the winter worked hard all spring and summer. In the fall, their first crops came in. The harvest was a success! They knew they'd be able to make it through the next winter thanks to God, hard work, and their Native American neighbors.

Before they left England, the Puritans had celebrated a good crop with a festival called a "Harvest Home." William Bradford, the Pilgrims' new governor, remembered this old tradition. During the fall of 1621, he declared that there would be a feast to celebrate their first bountiful harvest. Governor Bradford invited Chief Massasoit to come, as well. Together they would share the fruits of their labor.

The Pilgrims must have been surprised to see Chief Massasoit show up in Plymouth with 90 of his people! The four Pilgrim women

and two teenage girls who were doing the cooking might have been the most surprised of all. They had prepared several kinds of meat and fish, corn and pumpkin dishes, cranberries, and more. Still, there was not going to be enough food for so many. When the chief saw that more food would be needed, he sent some of his men out. They returned with five deer, turkeys, corn, squash, beans, and berries. It was a true potluck dinner!

. . . . . and Plant the Seed of Thanksgiving

The harvest celebration lasted for three days. Children played games such as hide-and-seek and blindman's-bluff. Everyone sang and danced. There were foot races and wrestling matches. The Pilgrim men had shooting contests to show off their skills with their weapons. The Native American men had bow-and-arrow contests to show off their skills with *their* weapons.

And everyone ate and ate and ate. Such bounty must have seemed a miracle after so many had died during that first tough winter.

Life would continue to be hard for the Pilgrims for many years to come. They all knew they had paid a high price for their freedom. But they had survived and were grateful for the chance to start a new life in a new world.

Today, we think of that wonderful harvest feast in 1621 as the first American Thanksgiving. (Although for the Native Americans, it was actually their fifth thanksgiving feast of the year!) The spirit of the Pilgrims' harvest feast was so powerful it has survived for almost 400 years. Even now, we celebrate the same things they did back in 1621: The bounty of the earth, the blessings of freedom, and fellowship among people.

The Pilgrims' first Harvest Home festival was the seed that eventually blossomed into the American Thanksgiving holiday we know today. This is the story of how it grew.

Thanksgiving

The travelers who arrived on the *Mayflower* brought the seed of Thanksgiving with them. But it would

The 17th Century: Thanksgiving Takes Root
(1600-1699)

Many Puritans followed the first Pilgrims to America. They brought another old tradition with them. This tradition was to proclaim special days of prayer and thanksgiving when something especially good happened. On those thanksgiving days, religious leaders would tell everyone to come to church to thank God for their good fortune.

Over time, thanksgiving days grew together with the Harvest Home. It was decided to have one big Thanksgiving celebration every year, right around harvest time. That way, the people could thank God for everything good that had happened during the year as they celebrated their harvest.

By the end of the 17th century, Thanksgiving Day had taken root. The governors of the colonies would pick a day of thanksgiving in the fall. Families would join together and go to church in the morning. Afterwards, they would come home for a big harvest feast, complete with turkey and pumpkin pie. Fun and games would follow. The kids would go outside and play. The adults would hold a big dance. Everyone in town would come to have a good time and enjoy the music.

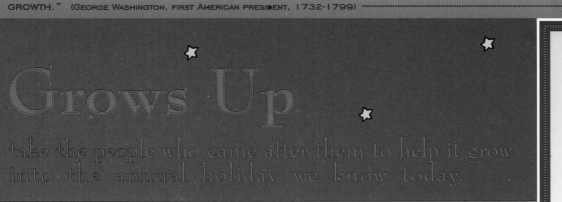

Grows Up

take the people who came after them to help it grow into the annual holiday we know today.

The 18th Century: A Thanksgiving Revolution
(1700-1799)

By the time the American Revolution took place in 1776, the Thanksgiving tradition was already well over one hundred years old! Before the revolution, each colony had celebrated Thanksgiving separately. When we became a single nation, we started to celebrate together.

After the war ended, George Washington was elected the first president of the new United Sates of America. When he became president in 1789, he urged Americans to give thanks for their hard-won freedom and their new Constitution. He understood how much our country had to be thankful for. He picked the last Thursday in November as a special national day of thanksgiving. That was the traditional date for the old New England holiday.

President Washington knew that there were many different kinds of Americans. He made sure his first national Thanksgiving proclamation included people of all beliefs and religions. Special Thanksgiving services were held in churches, synagogues, and meeting houses. Then families and friends went home for the traditional meal. The old Puritan tradition was now for everyone.

President Washington wanted Americans to be thankful, but he wasn't really trying to create an annual holiday for the whole country. It would take many more years and one very determined woman to make Thanksgiving a truly national celebration.

The 19th Century:
Thanksgiving Becomes a National Holiday
(1800-1899)

In the late 1820's, Sarah Josepha Hale wrote that Thanksgiving should be like the Fourth of July—a national holiday. In 1846, Mrs. Hale, a magazine editor and widowed mother of five, started a major campaign to make Thanksgiving a national holiday. She stated that Thanksgiving should be celebrated on the last Thursday of November. The country was growing bigger every day. She wanted everyone to enjoy Thanksgiving no matter where they lived. Mrs. Hale remembered the happy Thanksgivings she had spent as a little girl in New Hampshire. She also knew how much her own five children loved the holiday. Wouldn't it be nice, she thought, if all Americans could share the same wonderful experience?

Mrs. Hale used her magazine to teach her readers how to cook turkeys and prepare pumpkin pies and cranberry sauce—even if they had never seen a turkey in their lives! (Remember, there were no supermarkets in those days.) She published touching stories about families that had gathered from far and wide just for the holiday. She printed poems about boys and girls traveling through the fresh November snow to visit their grandparents. A poem describing this picturesque Thanksgiving was written by Lydia Maria Child, who knew Mrs. Hale. Her poem, *Over the River and Through the Wood*, was set to music and became Thanksgiving's unofficial anthem. We still love singing it today!

People enjoyed singing and reading about Thanksgiving. Just like today, families were often separated. Farm boys went off to the big city in search of their fortunes. Girls got married and moved away with their husbands. Lots of people were leaving eastern cities, towns, and farms to travel west. Her stories reminded everyone that it felt good to go home.

Mrs. Hale also helped people remember the story of the Pilgrims and how the country got started. The Pilgrims seemed brave, honest, religious, and independent. The old Thanksgiving story fit right in with how Americans thought of themselves. Before long, people from coast to

coast started to celebrate a New England Thanksgiving—even in places that had more buffalo than turkeys! Somehow the holiday made them feel like real Americans, no matter where they were.

For the next 20 years Mrs. Hale wrote letters to presidents, governors, and other important people urging them to make Thanksgiving an official national holiday. Finally, in 1863, in the middle of the Civil War, President Abraham Lincoln made an announcement. He announced that Thursday, November 26, would be a national day of

thanksgiving. He said that all presidents should continue every year to declare the fourth Thursday in November a holiday. Mrs. Hale had won her long battle. Over time, Americans took Thanksgiving into their hearts and welcomed it into their homes. Thanksgiving became a favorite national tradition.

Once, in 1939, President Franklin Delano Roosevelt tried to change the date of

Thanksgiving to make the Christmas shopping season longer. He wanted to move the holiday to the third week of November. Many Americans complained to their Congressmen. Two years later, in October 1941, Congress passed a law. The law stated that Thanksgiving would always be celebrated on the fourth Thursday in November. That's the date we celebrate today. Sarah Josepha Hale would certainly be proud. Her Thanksgiving dream has bridged America's past with America's present.

And it will continue to do so for generations to come.

The Great American

Because certain foods have been served on Thanksgiving for centuries, they have become

The most amazing thing about Thanksgiving dinner is that it's almost exactly the same today as it was at the first Thanksgiving feast! Chances are, your family eats pretty much the same foods eaten by the Pilgrims and their Native American neighbors. These foods were also enjoyed by George Washington, Sarah Hale, Abraham Lincoln, and Franklin D. Roosevelt. There are some differences, of course. For example, you probably don't have to chase your turkey through the woods before you cook it.

The idea of a big turkey dinner isn't new. When Mrs. Hale worked to make Thanksgiving a national holiday, the first thing she mentioned was the importance of the food. Her plan worked. No one could resist the idea of Thanksgiving dinner.

If you had lived back then, what would dinner have been like? Some things would be very different. But much would seem very familiar.

In the early 1800s, when Mrs. Hale lived, women always did the cooking. They were in charge of the kitchen. But everyone in the family helped out. The boys were sent outside to split firewood

Thanksgiving Feast

symbols of Thanksgiving. Each of these symbolic foods tells a story.

for the cast-iron stove and the big brick oven. Their job was to keep the fire going. The girls were put to work chopping and peeling and mashing. There were lost of fruits and vegetables to prepare. The men and older boys hunted deer, turkeys, and other meats.

The mothers and aunts and grandmothers would start cooking days in advance. They'd begin by baking pie after pie. Pumpkin, apple, cherry, and mincemeat were favorites. Then they'd make cranberry sauce, apple butter, and many kinds of spiced fruits.

Thanksgiving dinner in Mrs. Hale's time usually included corn, pumpkin, beans, squash, cranberries, turnips, onions, and mashed potatoes. And, of course, there was the big turkey. It was the centerpiece of the meal, just like it is today. They didn't stop there, though. In those days, they might have served a roast goose, a duck or two, a chicken pie, and even some beef! Can you imagine cooking, and eating, so much food? The custom was to put everything on the table at once. Even the fruit pies were considered part of the main meal. Do you like that idea?

The world has changed a lot since the days of Mrs. Hale. But the holiday meal has not. Turkey, corn, pumpkin pies, beans, cranberries, and happy families are still on the Thanksgiving menu.

What is the story behind these symbolic holiday foods?

THINK ABOUT IT: Table Manners

Even before the Pilgrim days, adults judged children by their manners. In fact, the Pilgrims had a book of manners that was full of rules, and the children had to learn and obey each and every one.

Do you want to be one of the most well-mannered children at your Thanksgiving feast? While it's not a book of manners, here are seven "Do's" and seven "Don't's" that should earn you much praise! Being well-mannered is also a perfect way to say "Thanks" to your family members for all they've done for you. Go ahead-make them proud!

1. DO dress up and brush up and wash up for dinner.
2. DO greet everyone and look them in the eye.
3. DO place your napkin on your lap and use it.
4. DO respond when someone speaks to you.
5. DO offer to help out and then cheerfully do what is asked.
6. DO say "PLEASE," "THANK YOU," and "EXCUSE ME" all day long!
7. DO compliment the foods you like!

1. DON'T begin eating until after the family blessing is said.
2. DON'T talk when your mouth is full.
3. DON'T interrupt when others are talking.
4. DON'T put your elbows on the table.
5. DON'T reach across the table.
6. DON'T get out of your seat (unless you are helping).
7. DON'T complain about the food (or anything else)!

There you go. Good table manners are as easy as 1, 2, 3, . . . 4, 5, 6, 7 . . . YOU can do it!

DO have a delicious and well-mannered Thanksgiving!

The Symbolism of Thanksgiving Foods

Turkey

Are you having turkey this Thanksgiving? If you are, you won't be alone. Turkey and Thanksgiving have gone together since the days of the Pilgrims. We know wild turkeys lived in New England. In fact, many people, including Benjamin Franklin, wanted to make the turkey the national bird instead of the bald eagle!

Domestic turkeys like the ones we eat today were brought to America by English settlers. (A domestic turkey is raised on a farm. A wild turkey lives in the woods.) The turkey's journey to North America began in Mexico. Spaniards brought turkeys to Europe from Mexico way back in 1519. When English settlers headed for North America, they brought turkeys with them. The gobbler sure has traveled a long way to get to your Thanksgiving feast!

🦃 The Turkey 🦃 and Its Wondrous Ways

Our language has changed a lot in a hundred years! In the time of Mrs. Hale, children often read and understood English written like this:

A truly superb and interesting creature is the turkey, whether we view him with the eyes of . . . the artist or the small boy who meets him alone in a narrow path. It is a brave small boy who dares face the irate majesty of a full-grown gobbler.

I say he is superb. Observe him as he swells and struts, the crowned king of the barnyard, showing the subdued magnificence of his plumage to the October sun!
(from The Youth's Companion, November 22, 1883)

Corn

Corn, or maize, was the first of the Indian Three Sisters. It is native to America. Corn came in many varieties—red, white, blue, and yellow. Native Americans may have been growing it for hundreds of years before Europeans arrived. The Pilgrims had never seen it in England. It was new to their diet, but they might have starved without it. Corn was certainly part of their first harvest festival. Today, when we prepare sweet corn and cornbread, it reminds us of the importance of corn to the Pilgrims' survival. The corn we eat is much bigger than the small, multicolored cobs the Native Americans grew. Nevertheless, Indian corn has become a symbol of the harvest and our long and wonderful Thanksgiving heritage.

Cornhusk dolls, like these, have been made for centuries. Native American parents used the husks from corn to make dolls for their children. Pilgrims learned to make these dolls, too. The cornhusk dolls are made out of dried husks from fresh corn on the cob. The dolls' hair is made from dried inner white and outer brown threads, called corn silk.

RECIPE: Easy Cornbread

1 cup cornmeal (white, blue, or yellow)
1 egg
1 cup flour (white and/or whole wheat)
1 cup milk
1/4 cup vegetable oil
3 to 4 tablespoons sugar
1 tablespoon baking powder
1/2 teaspoon salt (optional)

Preheat oven to 425 degrees. (Get an adult to help.)
Grease a 9-inch square cake pan with butter.

To make:
In a big bowl, stir together the cornmeal, the flour, the sugar, the baking powder, and the salt.
Beat the egg in a little bowl, then add it to the dry ingredients.
Then add the milk and the oil and stir them in very well until the batter is smooth.
Pour the batter into the greased baking pan.
Put it into the oven and bake for 20-25 minutes.
(Get an adult to help you take it out of the oven when it's done.)
Let the cornbread cool in the pan and cut it into squares.

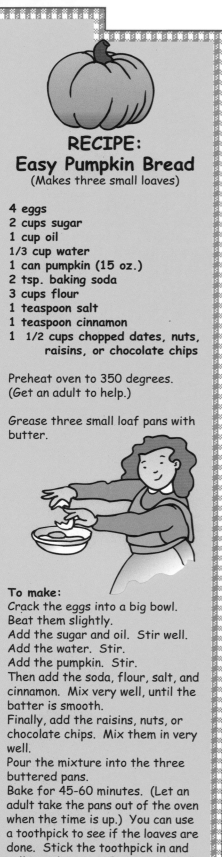

RECIPE:
Easy Pumpkin Bread
(Makes three small loaves)

4 eggs
2 cups sugar
1 cup oil
1/3 cup water
1 can pumpkin (15 oz.)
2 tsp. baking soda
3 cups flour
1 teaspoon salt
1 teaspoon cinnamon
1 1/2 cups chopped dates, nuts,
      raisins, or chocolate chips

Preheat oven to 350 degrees.
(Get an adult to help.)

Grease three small loaf pans with butter.

To make:
Crack the eggs into a big bowl.
Beat them slightly.
Add the sugar and oil. Stir well.
Add the water. Stir.
Add the pumpkin. Stir.
Then add the soda, flour, salt, and cinnamon. Mix very well, until the batter is smooth.
Finally, add the raisins, nuts, or chocolate chips. Mix them in very well.
Pour the mixture into the three buttered pans.
Bake for 45-60 minutes. (Let an adult take the pans out of the oven when the time is up.) You can use a toothpick to see if the loaves are done. Stick the toothpick in and pull it right out. If it's completely dry, the bread is done. If it's gooey, put the loaves back in for a few more minutes.
When they're done, let them cool on a rack, then turn the pans over and let the loaves fall out.

Pumpkin and squash together were the second of the Indian Three Sisters. The Pilgrims were introduced to the pumpkin by their Native American neighbors, and it has been a part of Thanksgiving ever since.

Although we don't eat pumpkin very often anymore, the first Americans ate it all the time. Pumpkins were easy to grow and would last a long time in the cellar during winter. That was important in the days before refrigerators.

Puritan children could expect to see pumpkin at breakfast, lunch, and dinner. There was pumpkin sauce, pumpkin custard, pumpkin pudding, and, of course, pumpkin pie. The all-American pumpkin has been a Thanksgiving favorite for just about 400 years!

A delightful, old Native American legend describes the three sisters this way: The eldest sister is the Spirit of the Corn. She wears silken tassels which rustle as she moves. The sister called the Spirit of the Bean wears clinging green leaves. She clings to and leans on her older sister for support. The youngest sister is the Spirit of the Squash and Pumpkin. She wears a golden crown and sits at the feet of her older sisters.

Beans

Beans were the third of the Indian Three Sisters. These Native American beans were called pole beans, because their stems need to cling to a pole for support. That is why Squanto taught the Pilgrims to plant the beans next to cornstalks. As the beans grew, they used the cornstalks as their poles.

Beans are frequently served at Thanksgiving. People who don't eat turkey or other meat often serve several types of beans, since beans combined with other foods are a great source of protein. A popular Native American dish called succotash combines the Indian Three Sisters to simmer together in the same pot.

Cranberries

Cranberries should have been a fourth Indian Sister! Cranberries were originally called "crane berries" because the plant's pink blossoms looked like a crane's head. They grew wild in bogs along the New England coast. They are a great source of vitamin C, which the Pilgrims desperately needed during their journey and their first winter in America. Unfortunately, they didn't know about cranberries until Squanto arrived. He showed the Pilgrims where to find them and how to dry them for the winter. The vitamin C in cranberries might have saved the many people who died from scurvy during that first brutal winter.

As soon as the Pilgrims figured out how to sweeten the bitter little berries with maple sugar, they started making cranberry sauce. (Squanto showed them how to make maple sugar with sap from maple trees.) Cranberry sauce has been turkey's favorite Thanksgiving partner ever since.

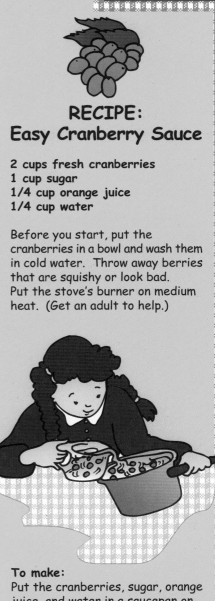

RECIPE:
Easy Cranberry Sauce

2 cups fresh cranberries
1 cup sugar
1/4 cup orange juice
1/4 cup water

Before you start, put the cranberries in a bowl and wash them in cold water. Throw away berries that are squishy or look bad. Put the stove's burner on medium heat. (Get an adult to help.)

To make:
Put the cranberries, sugar, orange juice, and water in a saucepan on medium heat.
Stir gently for 7 to 10 minutes, until all the cranberries pop open.
Let the mixture cool for a few minutes.
Then pour it into a serving bowl and put it in the refrigerator to chill.
Remember to turn off the stove.

Sharing the Thanksgiving Bounty

Thanksgiving has always been a time for families to get together. It has also been a time when families share the bounty of the Thanksgiving feast with people less fortunate than themselves. The Puritans would always bake extra pies and roast extra turkeys for their poorer neighbors. Children would be sent out with baskets stuffed with food to make sure everyone in the community would have a nice Thanksgiving dinner.

This Thanksgiving tradition of sharing has continued for hundreds of years. During the Civil War families would set a place at their table for soldiers who couldn't get to their own homes. Families also made room for widows whose husbands had died in the war. In the late 1800s, big banquets were often given at orphanages, hospitals, and prisons. Today, Thanksgiving dinners are also served to elderly and homeless Americans.

Putting the "Thanks" Back Into Thanksgiving!

What do you have to be thankful for this year? (Are you thankful for your health? For your family? Are you grateful you're an American?) There are many ways to give thanks at Thanksgiving. One of the most traditional ways is to say grace before the meal. It has been part of Thanksgiving celebrations since the Pilgrim days. Grace is a small prayer that offers thanks to God for the bounty of the feast and for the loved ones gathered to eat it. In many families, grace is a time to review the good things that have happened during the past year. It is also an opportunity to express hopes for happiness and peace for the coming year.

THINK ABOUT IT: The Gift of Giving

Can you think of ways you can share the bounty of Thanksgiving with others? The Thanksgiving tradition of giving often helps us feel grateful for what we have. Try making the pumpkin flower vase or candle applesticks below as a gift for someone you know who could use some holiday cheer. Make sure that a parent is with you when you deliver your thoughtful gift.

Applesticks:

You will need:
Two large apples, an apple corer, a small knife, two tapered candles, a lemon, and two pieces of aluminum foil.

To make:
Core the apple halfway to make room for the candle. Squeeze lemon on any design you make to keep it from turning brown. Put the applesticks, candles, and foil in a bag. When you and your parent deliver your gift, place the apples on the foil and the candles in the applesticks.

Pumpkin Flower Vase:

You will need:
A medium-sized pumpkin, knife, big spoon, water, cut flowers.

To make:
Have an adult cut off the top of the pumpkin. With the big spoon, scoop out the pumpkin seeds and the walls of the pumpkin. (You can wash and save the seeds to bake later!) Place the flowers in the pumpkin. When you and your parent deliver the vase, fill it halfway with water.

Put your "thanks" back into Thanksgiving!

On this Thanksgiving Day 2_____ I want to give thanks for . . .

I AM THANKFUL FOR THIS YUMMY DINNER.

Thanksgiving

While the turkey is cooking, families have always found lots of ways to have fun together. Many families play ball, cards, and board games. Other families go for walks. When dinner

Games, Sports, and Fun

Way back in the 1700s in wintry New England, boys and girls would go outside after the big Thanksgiving meal. With full stomachs, the children went skating on frozen ponds or sledding down snowy hills. Later, families would play games such as charades, chess, or checkers, or listen to children recite poetry. In the early 1800s, mothers and fathers and boys and girls would go out to see big parades or bonfires. Some towns even had fireworks. Thanksgiving Day parades are still a holiday tradition in many cities and towns.

Does anyone in your family go outside and throw a football around on Thanksgiving Day? If they do, they're part of an American tradition that dates all the way back to the Civil War. In the 1860s and 1870s, local football (and baseball) teams would hold contests on Thanksgiving Day. By the 1880s, college football games were already a holiday tradition. Not everyone approved of this. Many people worried that playing or watching football on Thanksgiving took away from the central points of the holiday; family and religion. Some people still think this today. But, for many, games and sports are part of what makes Thanksgiving special. What games, sports, and fun are shared by your family?

Traditions

is over and the dishes are done, some families tell stories, read aloud, sing , dance, perform, or play outside. These are all age-old Thanksgiving traditions.

American Music

American music has always been an important part of Thanksgiving celebrations. What is American music? Where does it come from? Not surprisingly, several types of music from many countries, cultures, peoples, and religions have contributed to the creation of American music. Some of these types are ballads, hymns, Native American music, and spirituals.

Ballads are songs that tell a story about life, love, family, or work. Ballads came to America with the European settlers from countries such as England, Scotland, and Ireland.   Hymns, or songs of praise, also came to America with the European settlers. Hymns were usually sung in church, and frequently came from older songs like psalms. Native American music was first heard by the settlers after they became acquainted with their new neighbors. Some tribes believed that all songs were created by their gods at the beginning of time. Spirituals are songs that were sung by black Africans who had been taken to America. Spirituals combine African chants with hymns. Like hymns, spirituals were often sung in groups.

Before the days of television, music was a big part of home life in America. With the whole family assembled from far and wide, Thanksgiving was a natural time for group singing, music making, dancing, and having family fun. Everyone would gather around the hearth to sing and play their favorite tunes. What American songs do you and your family sing on Thanksgiving? How about *Over the River and Through the Wood*?

Over the River and Through the Wood
by Lydia Maria Child

Mrs. Child's poem was first published in 1840. It was later set to a traditional French folk tune, and soon became Thanksgiving's unofficial anthem.

O-ver the riv-er and through the wood, To grandfather's house we go; ------ The horse knows the way to car-ry the sleigh, through the white and drift-ed snow. -----

O-ver the riv-er and through the wood. - Oh, how the wind does blow! ------- It stings the toes, and bites the nose, As o-ver the ground we go.

2. Over the river and through the wood
Trot fast my dapple-gray!
Spring over the ground
Like a hunting-hound!
For 'tis Thanksgiving Day.

3. Over the river and through the wood,
And straight through the barnyard gate.
We seem to go
Extremely slow --
It is so hard to wait!

4. Over the river and through the wood, --
Now grandmother's cap I spy!
Hurrah for the fun!
Is the pudding done?
Hurrah for the pumpkin pie!

Thanksgiving has changed a lot since that first harvest celebration. But its spirit of community and family togetherness has never changed!